BODY TO EARTH

Three Artists From Brazil

Cildo Meireles

Mario Cravo Neto

Tunga

Guest Curator:
Susan M. Anderson

January 13 - February 20, 1993

Fisher Gallery
University of Southern California

Body to Earth

Guest Curator: Susan M. Anderson

© 1992 Fisher Gallery
University of Southern California

ISBN: 0-945192-10-X

Library of Congress Catalog Card Number 92-73010

All rights reserved. No part of this catalogue may be reproduced in any form by an electronic or mechanical means including information storage and retrieval systems without permission in writing from the Fisher Gallery except by a reviewer who may quote brief passages in review.

This exhibition and catalogue are supported in part by a grant from the National Endowment for the Arts, a Federal agency. Travel provided by Varig Brazilian Airlines.

Printer: Pearl River Printing Company, Hong Kong

Design/Production: Jerome Sander

Quantity: 1000

Fisher Gallery
University of Southern California
University Park
Los Angeles, CA 90089-0292

Photo Credits
Luiz Alphonsus: 6, 12
Mario Cravo Neto: 17-25
Pedro Oswaldo Cruz: 7, 8
Jilles Huthinson: cover, 31, 32, 33
Kanaal Art Foundation: 13
Renato La Clete: 10
Wilton Montenegro: cover, 9, 11, 14, 15, 35
James Prinz: 30
Miguel Rio Branco: 28

FISHER GALLERY

Accredited by the American Association of Museums

Preface and Acknowledgements

Since Guest Curator Susan M. Anderson's first research trip to Brazil in 1989 on a planning grant from the National Endowment for the Arts, Brazil has experienced several dramatic turn of events which have riveted the eyes of the world on the country. In 1989 the Brazilian people voted in a new president, Fernando Collar de Mello, the first freely elected leader in three decades. One of his first acts was to freeze the economy, instituting severe austerity policies and causing many to leave Brazil seeking better economic conditions. In June 1992 the country hosted the United Nations Conference on the Environment and Development—the "Earth Summit." Also in June 1992, five Brazilian artists were invited to exhibit in Documenta IX in Kassel—a high number of artists from one country (i.e. six French artists participated). In October a Brazilian congressional panel, under dramatic pressure of the people, impeached President Collar on corruption charges—thus signalling a new era for Brazil.

The idea for an exhibition of Brazilian art originated in 1988 with Susan Anderson, Curator of Exhibitions, Laguna Art Museum and alumna of USC's Museum Studies Program, and former Exhibitions Coordinator at Fisher Gallery, Georgia Freedman-Harvey. A devoted partisan of Brazilian art, Susan Anderson had spent considerable time in Brazil and knew the language and culture of the country. Fisher Gallery submitted and received a research grant in 1988 and an implementation grant in 1991 from the NEA. During the first phase of the project, Brazilian curator Cecilia Ribeiro acted as a research assistant in Brazil, helping to put the Guest Curator in contact with artists and facilitating communication between the two countries. Many others went out of their way to help the Guest Curator in the organization of the exhibition or on her two research trips to Brazil, providing hospitality, friendly support, as well as research assistance: Carlos Guilherme Mota, Adriana Lopez, Fernando and Caterina Silva, Marcio Doctors, Luiza Rotbart, Andrea Tonacci, Luiz Rosemburg Filho, Dado and Silvinha Aguiar, Afonso Costa, Franklin Pedroso, Ivan Kudrna, Regina Eusey, Luiza Strina, Paulo Herkenhoff, Jac Leirner and Fernanda Gomes. Others who were especially generous during the organization of the exhibition were Edward Leffingwell and Guy Brett. Cecilia Ribeiro and Bolton Colburn read drafts of the catalogue and made helpful suggestions, while Charles Desmarais generously edited the manuscript. Heidi Nikisher accurately compiled the biographies and bibliography. Mari Carmen Ramírez, Curator of Latin American Art, and Beverly Adams, Assistant Curator at the Archer M. Huntington Art Gallery, University of Texas at Austin, were especially helpful as well as Elaine Lipson, Assistant Curator, Museum of Contemporary Art in Chicago, and Bruce Guenther, Curator, Newport Harbor Art Museum, Newport Beach. Thanks are also in order for Paulo A.V. Wolowski, Deputy Counsellor for Brazil, for his help in securing funds for the exhibition and to M. Espirito Santo, Banco de Brasil, Los Angeles. Finally, we extend our appreciation to Cicero Cavalheiro whose advice was always useful to the Gallery.

The untiring staff of Fisher Gallery supported the project in every way possible, recognizing the importance of the exhibition and exercising great patience in the face of the many difficulties which arise in the organization of an international exhibition. To them, I owe my sincere thanks: Kay Allen, Associate Director; Jennifer Jaskowiak, Exhibitions Coordinator and Collections Manager; Sherrie Ray, Education Coordinator; Scott Chamberlin, Preparator; and Rhonda Howard, Administrative Assistant.

Selma Holo
Director, Fisher Gallery

Susan M. Anderson
Guest Curator

Introduction

Many years ago, the writer and environmentalist Wallace Stegner referred to the American West as "the native home of hope."[1] Brazil is considered now by many the new land of hope and a paradise with limitless opportunites. Envisioned as Edens, both California and Brazil labor under and exploit many of the same myths. Both are beautifully endowed, the one arid but fertile, the other exotic, fecund, tropical. As frontier territories, the Western U.S. and Brazil are warehouses of all sorts of wealth, warehouses that have been plundered and exploited. The economic system that allows this situation shows no concern for the environment or its inhabitants, or for the labor force used for the exploitation, or even for its own sustainability. According to Stegner, California "encourages a fatal carelessness, a destructiveness, because it seems so limitless."[2] It is clear that California has come to the limit of that limitlessness. And so has Brazil.

California and Brazil are plagued by problems of social unrest, overpopulation, limited resources, pollution. In an attempt to feed and shelter its exploding population and to bolster its failed economy, Brazil is consuming irreplaceable natural resources at an alarming rate. But while the U.S. points the finger at Brazil on such issues as deforestation, it fails to admit that much of the development in the rainforests has been by foreign interests furthering their own economic ambitions. And because of Brazil's huge external debt, the country remains economically dependent on, and beholden to, the U.S.

Deep, underlying tensions between North and South America became clear during the United Nations Conference on the Environment and Development—the "Earth Summit"—held in Rio de Janeiro in June 1992. The relaxation of cold war tensions and the heightening of a global ecological crisis fostered awareness of the pressing need to confront worldwide environmental concerns, including poverty, underdevelopment and the consumption of paradise. The confrontation between the industrial and the ecological is now one of the major issues of our time.

Artistic expression has the ability to symbolize complex abstractions in concrete ways, and the potential to raise social and economic consciousness. Brazil and California (especially the city of Los Angeles) both suffer the multiple consequences of the philosophy of domination—whether social, economic or environmental—and both regions are now producing art which can be seen as a response to crisis.

Much of the most advanced contemporary Brazilian art of the last forty years has reflected these same concerns. Beginning in the 1950s, the Brazilian avant-garde initiated an emanicipatory process, the reverberations of which are felt today. In this, Brazilian art history parallels that of the U.S., a country whose own artistic awakening occurred after World War II. Whereas in the U.S. that awakening was to Abstract Expressionism, in Brazil the trend was toward Geometric Abstraction.[3]

Geometric Abstraction, rooted in the art of Mondrian, Malevich and the Russian Constructivists, came to interest Brazilian artists about the same time it did artists in Southern California—that is, when New York and San Francisco were experiencing the Abstract Expressionist boom and Paris was involved in Tachism, l'Art Brut and l'Art Informal. In Rio de Janeiro in 1959, the intellectually and conceptually powerful Neo-Concrete movement was born. Its main players—Lygia Clark, Helio Oiticica, Lygia Pape and Amilcar de Castro—translated the language of geometric abstraction and the social engagement of Constructivism into their own language, preserving an openness and receptivity to the political and social world in which they lived.[4]

Brazil was then going through great social transformations, as well as undertaking the processes of industrialization and urbanization. The cultural explosion of the 1950s affected all the arts, offering Brazil a rational new face, a new social direction. It included not only the Neo-Concrete movement in the visual arts, but the modern architectural forms which resulted in the city of Brasilia, the Brazilian jazz form Bossa Nova and Cinema Novo.

The legacy of these conceptual artists, particularly that of Helio Oiticica and Lygia Clark, is most visible in contemporary installation works which, more often than not, reflect both international art issues and those of contemporary Brazilian society. The attitudinal stance of the three artists in this exhibition, Mario Cravo Neto, Cildo Meireles and Tunga, in varying degrees, is similar to that first proposed by the Neo-Concrete movement, and by Oiticica in particular: "a thought in expansion, a form of social action, a type of politics."[5] The Brazilian critic Frederico Morais called Oiticica's work "a programme, a vision of the world, an ethic."[6] According to the English critic Guy Brett, Oiticica and Clark proposed an art of "life-acts" and "behavior," an art which could be exported anywhere, taken up by others and mixed with local cultural possibilities.[7] Oiticica's "radical marginality" led him to "consider art as a form of revolt against every form of oppression: intellectual, aesthetic, metaphysical or, especially, social."[8]

The Rio artists' Neo-Concrete Manifesto (1959) adopted the geometric and social concerns of Constructivism but not its mechanistic side: "If we have to look for an equivalent to the work of art, we will not find it in the machine, or even the object as such, but...in living organisms."[9] The body, a particulary important theme for Lygia Clark, has also been a recurring metaphor in the work of the artists in this exhibition. By the early 1960s Clark was using her own body or those of others. "Her 'sculptures' had become simple, flexible, somewhat organic devices made of rubber bands, polythene, air, stones and so on, which were to be handled, worn, or passed from one person to another. So convinced did Lygia Clark become of the efficacy of her insights into the relationship between the physical and metaphorical in the body's experience, that towards the end of her life she actually used her devices in a therapeutic treatment for people with mental disturbances."[10] Clark proposed a kind of intervention in the patterns of time and space. Meireles's early work such as his *Insertions into Ideological Circuits*, a politicized version of this, has had an equally profound influence on later Brazilian artists.

Mario Cravo Neto, Cildo Meireles and Tunga are roughly of one generation—that following the explosive artistic experimentation of the Neo-Concrete movement. There is no one thing that conveniently ties their work together except that it penetrates some of the key directions and issues of contemporary Brazilian art and society. Each has also melded a unique combination of art discourse, interdisciplinary study and social concerns. Each also has an acute awareness of the natural environment. Through their work one comes in contact with the ecological reality of the country: the vastness of the geography, the seemingly limitless natural resources, the rich heritage of the native, Portuguese and Afro-Brazilian cultures. Juxtaposed to this is the paradoxical reality that the natural resources, native cultures and even nature itself are finite, and disappearing. These artists envision a sense of history grounded upon an ethical perspective. They explore the concepts of the domination of cultures and of discovery, offering us insight into our own urges to claim new territory. They incorporate the mystery and sublimity of Brazil's natural environment and its various cultures into their art to reclaim them for the future.

A sense of the sublime permeates the work, as does the tension between elemental order and chaos. The quality of the sublime in a work of art is said to inspire awe tinged with horror—a state of mind equivalent to a religious experience—usually because of an intrinsic elevated quality. These artists create something profound and disturbing of a corporal and telluric, rather than celestial, order.

In spite of the qualities of the strange and the marvelous, which demand of the viewer an intense involvement with emotions of the sublime, the work maintains a poise between exuberance and stillness, superficiality and depth, erudition and mundaneness, order and chaos. It is addressed to a contemporary international culture which is nourished by the macabre, one that is losing its sense of survival for the species, destroying not only ecological systems but whole human and animal populations as well.

The Consumption of Paradise

> "I remember that in 1968-69-70... we were already no longer working with metaphors (representations) of situations. We were working with situations themselves, real...To work no longer with the metaphor of gunpowder—but to work with the gunpowder itself." [1]
>
> —Cildo Meireles

Cildo Meireles

Tiradentes: Totem – Monument to the Political Prisoner, 1970
Location: Belo Horizonte, Minas Gerais

In 1968, when Brazilian artist Cildo Meireles began making his first overtly political work, Brazil was at the height of a 20-year military dictatorship that strictly, and often violently, controlled such standard means of communication as radio, television, film, newspapers and other printed materials.[2] *Tiradentes: Totem— Monumento ao Preso Politico (Tiradentes: Totem— Monument to the Political Prisoner)* was Meireles's most direct response to the political climate and it expressed his personal despair. He created the piece in Belo Horizonte in 1970 for an exhibition inaugurating the new Palacio das Artes.

Meireles put up a wooden stake and surrounded it with a white cloth. He took ten living chickens, tied them to the stake and, dousing the chickens with gasoline, set them on fire. Still uncomfortable with the memory of this act, Meireles remembers that for many who witnessed the event, the explosion recalled the well-televised image of Buddhist monks who created a funeral pyre for themselves during the Vietnam War. Meireles was, in fact, making reference to the martyrs of the 1792 conspiracy led by Tiradentes (the hero of Brazilian independence who was captured and cruelly hung, drawn and quartered), thereby throwing attention on those imprisoned and tortured for dissent in his own time. Two days later, the government publicly denounced Meireles's act at an official ceremony.

Tiradentes: Totem was a radical artistic manifestation which violently and dramatically symbolized Meireles's opposition to political events. More often Meireles's artistic acts were unobtrusive, albeit potent, interventions integrated into the pattern of his daily life. Because censorship made it impossible to publicly protest government policy, Meireles ingeniously devised alternate modes of communication. In one of these projects, *Insertions into Ideological Circuits: Coca-Cola Project*, 1970, he silkscreened subversive messages onto the sides of returnable Coca-Cola bottles (the most well-known was "yankees go home!") which he then reinserted back into social circulation via the deposit system.

Meireles chose the quintessentially Yankee symbol of the Coca-Cola bottle to carry his message for particular reasons. During the military regime, there was rapid growth in Brazil, due in large part to the "sale" of the country to foreign powers such as the

Insertions into Ideological Circuits: Coca-Cola Project, 1970
Screenprinting on Coca-Cola bottles

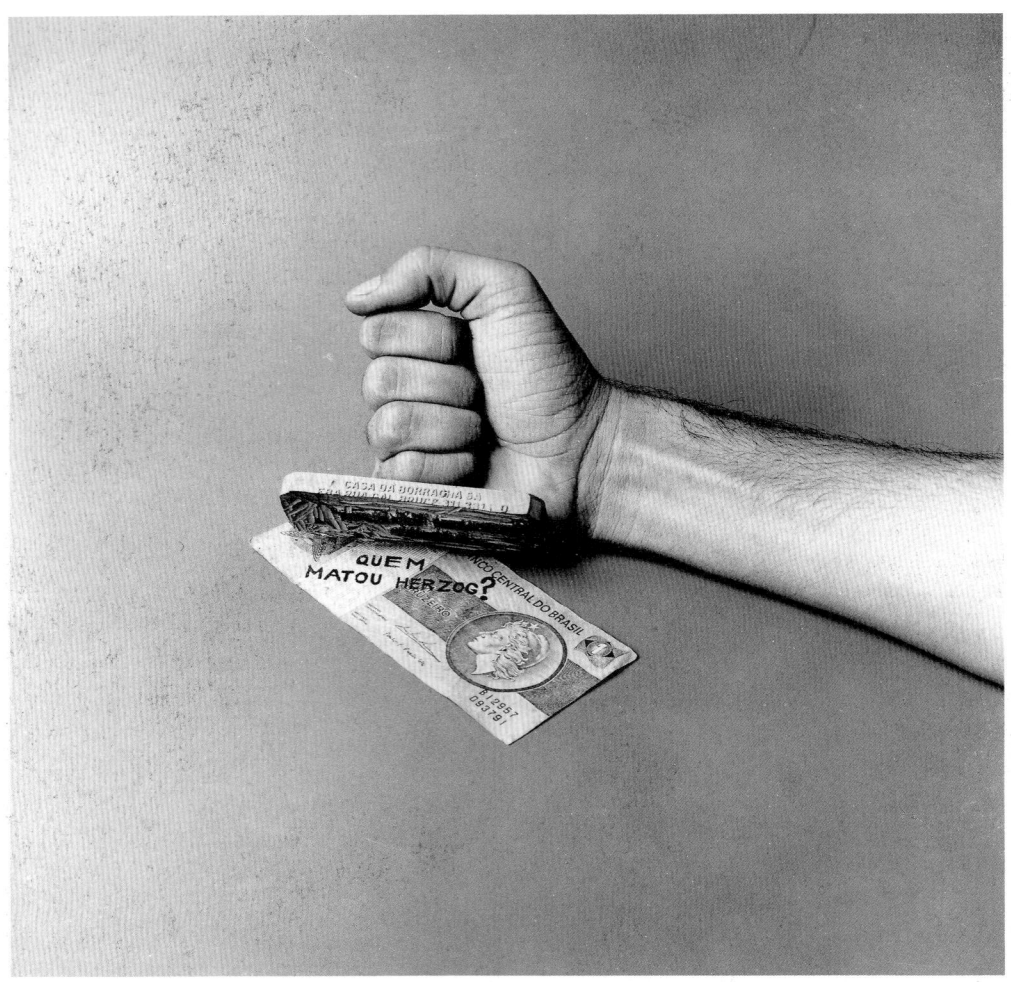

Insertions into Ideological Circuits: Banknote Project, 1970
Stamp on banknotes

U.S., which poured money into Brazil and helped finance the military takeover.

Meireles was both courageous in presenting politically "hot" work at this time and prescient as he anticipated changes in art which would appear sometime later. When the Museum of Modern Art in New York invited him to show the Coca-Cola bottles in the 1970 exhibition *Information*, few artists internationally were creating politically conceptual work—most were interested in purely formal, process and perceptual questions.[3]

Although Meireles's work from this period is an excellent early example of the interaction between conceptualism and political activism in the social sphere, it is also a brilliant extension of Pop art, which appropriates and transforms images made popular through consumer use. Meireles's practice of taking objects in and out of ideological and social circuits is a direction in Brazilian art that has been, and is being, fully exploited by artists of a younger generation in Brazil such as Jac Leirner. Though much of contemporary Brazilian art makes reference to mass culture, it usually refers to the culture of the lower classes, not the middle class or consumer class as is customary in the U.S. This trend can be equated with "the struggle for a voice."[4]

Meireles's body of work comprises two lines which, although nearly distinct, are closely related and interdependent. They intersect each other freely and frequently. One line has been concerned chiefly with formal and perceptual questions—with the philosophy of meaning. In a series of works spanning many years called *Eureka/Blindhotland*, 1970-1975, Meireles explored the limits of perception and art, fusing both within a context of conceptual issues. In these installations, he addressed

Eureka/Blindhotland, 1970-1975
Installation, São Paulo
Wood; 200 black rubber balls, each one a different weight; nylon net;
felt; 8 plates for newspaper insertions; 9 sound tracks of falling balls

the profound distance between appearance and reality. Works of this line are aligned with the world of thought and order.

The other line, the focus of this essay, has social and political dimensions. It expresses the experience of the Brazilian people and their culture, the violence of the streets, chaos. This line of work grows out of human experience and the artist's own struggle for a voice.

Meireles's work also heightens tensions between order and chaos, spareness and excess, geometric purity and organic decay. His work is about the relation of opposites, the interaction of fine art and the culture of the masses, the tension between the inevitability of death and the urge for self-preservation.

Like *Tiradentes* and *Insertions into Ideological Circuits*, much of Meireles's recent work is about the clash or tension between official and unofficial culture. Unlike *Tiradentes*, however, it exudes an atmosphere of calm, and only portends the possibility of repression and violence. In *Missão/Missões (How to Build Cathedrals)*, recreated for Fisher Gallery, Meireles's politics, in the words of Lawrence Wechsler, "are more ambiguous, less polemical, more steeped in a sense of the tragic dimensions of the issues he addresses."[5] Meireles's recent work "invites stillness and thought in dealing with violent and chaotically fluctuating reality."[6]

How to Build Cathedrals is a haven into which we may enter but which gives us no peace—a circular space, like the sacred space of the Church, but one also recalling the habitational and ritual spaces of indigenous cultures. It is

Tree of Money, 1969
Bound Brazilian banknotes

How to Build Cathedrals, 1987
Installation, São Paulo
600,000 coins; 2000 bones; 800 Communion hosts;
86 stone slabs; black jersey

Sermon on the Mount: Fiat Lux, 1973/1979
Installation, Rio de Janeiro
126,000 matchboxes; mirrors; sandpaper floor; sound track; actors
Duration: 24 hours

dark, primordial, shrouded in ambiguity. A reminder of death, like an enormous Catholic reliquary. The Brazilian firm Iochpe originally commissioned the installation in 1987 for *Missions—300 years,* an exhibition that examined the historical episode of the Jesuit missions in Brazil.

As in his earlier work, Meireles is here concerned with symbolic inversions, implicit in the kinds of materials he uses. The bones (numbering some 2,000) are simultaneously tokens of life and death and, because they are the bones of cattle, suggestive of the exploitation of the Brazilian rainforest to produce meat for exportation. Cattle raising, among other industries, has forced the Indians off the land and is leading to their extermination Since the first European contact, native populations have declined from eight million to less than 200,000 today. Meireles suggests that the first world is built on the bones of others.

The communion host is simultaneously a symbol of consumption and a token of Catholic devotion, redemption and miracle. In Roman Catholicism the blessed host is the body of Christ. Lu Menezes called this column of 800 wafers linking the bones to the coins "an invisible inflation of the body," like a spine or central cortex.[7]

The money, Meireles's signature material since 1969, is symbolic of the transience of life and also recalls the dizzying inflation of Brazil. The heavenly glitter of some 600,000 coins symbolizes the greed that has threatened, and still

12

threatens, the country's natural resources as well as the native peoples of Brazil.

The problem of the extermination of native peoples in Brazil is extremely complex. Poor are pitted against poor. According to Meireles: "In 1950, 70 percent of Brazilians lived in the countryside, with only 30 percent in the cities. The great majority of Brazilians subsisted by farming their meagre plots. But over the years the big landowners swallowed up more and more of those plots, expelling the peasants, often at gunpoint, and converting their lands to monoculture—oranges for example, or cattle, usually for export. This year [1989] we're doing a new census and we expect 85 percent of Brazilians will be seen to be living in the cities, the vast majority of those in truly wretched *favelas* [shanty towns]. Some, however, instead move deeper and deeper into the hinterlands, out of desperation, where of course they begin encountering Indians who've been living there for centuries. And soon you begin seeing these terrible massacres."[8]

Meireles has always been close to the problems of the native Brazilian due to his upbringing. When Meireles was a child, his father, a government official in Goias, was the first to expose a government scandal involving a case of genocide. In 1930, virus-bearing clothes had been

Through, 1989
Installation, Kortrijk, Belgium
Mixed media

intentionally thrown out of planes to the Crao tribe so that their native land could be commercially exploited. (A simple cold is enough to wipe out an entire tribe.) Many of the survivors became beggars or crazy. Ten years later the same tribe was attacked in their sleep and massacred with machine guns.

Meireles's uncle, Chico Meireles, was a famous explorer—a *sertanista*—who, during the 1940s and 1950s, was one of the first to try to save the Indians from inevitable extinction by helping them to gain economic control of their lands. Apoena Meireles, Chico's son, carried on his father's work and eventually set up one of the first national parks and Indian preserves, in Aripuana.

In pondering the implications of this background on Meireles's work, one can't help but think of a few lines written by the artist:

All I know is that being ephemeral
is very different from being disposable.
Being ephemeral is a metaphysical condition,
based on the hypothesis that the universe is finite.
While being disposable is a mode of economic
consumerism, founded on the illusion of infinity. [9]

Meireles very early on saw a need for a radical reevaluation of the institutions and ideologies associated with the dominator model of culture. He suggests the need for a new definition of culture to counteract that proposed by industry and technology, which act only in consideration of immediate supply and demand. He questions the symbolic codes of consumption, along with the waste, ecocide and global crisis he identifies with contemporary capitalism.

How to Build Cathedrals, 1987
Detail of floor

How to Build Cathedrals, 1987
Detail of ceiling

Scars of Our Inheritance

Mario Cravo Neto

Voodoo Figure, 1988, is the brooding study of a crouched figure splattered with opaque whitewash, fingers interlaced around bowed head, body a human canvas. The title of the photograph makes reference to nocturnal mysteries; its subject recalls the artist's memory of workmen whitewashing his childhood home. The picture reveals Mario Cravo Neto's mastery of nuance and sculptural form. As Edward Leffingwell has put it: "Cravo Neto's subjects have an almost muscular authority, and their dark richness is not decorative but brooding and somehow spiritual."[1]

Cravo Neto's work exemplifies an intangible link with spiritual forces in the same way that Afro-Brazilian ritual codifies a link with the deities or *Orixas*. The artist charges his photographs with mystical energy, expressing a state of mind not unlike a religious experience. His human subjects hide or mask their faces, whether with living creatures or objects of aesthetic and liturgical power. Once masked, his subjects take on ritual identities. Secret, essential natures become visible, individual personalities disappear. In creating a synthetic expression of the relationship between cultures in tropical Brazil, Cravo Neto subverts any ethnographic possibility using ambiguity, amplifying the sense of mystical introspection in his pictures. Although highly charged with the exoticism of the Afro-Brazilian culture, the work equally invokes the magic of tribal shamans and the baroque sensibility of the Portuguese culture of Brazil.

Mario Cravo Neto is a sculptor and photographer living in São Salvador da Bahia, the capital of Bahia, Brazil's largest and most impoverished state. Located on the coast in the northeast of the country, Bahia was the principal center for the importation of slaves by the Portuguese in the sixteenth century. The city's mixture of indigenous, Portuguese and African populations makes Bahia heir to a rich cultural heritage unique in Latin America.

According to Cravo Neto, his photography incorporates the facial expressions, gestures and ritual objects characteristic of the racial groups making up the population of Bahia.[2] Although he does not make anthropological photography—rather a highly personal form of psychological portraiture—Cravo Neto is very close to the circle of photographer-ethnographers who have made a study of indigenous tribal and African culture in Brazil. Included in this circle are Maureen Bisilliat and the

Voodoo Figure, 1988
Photograph

Untitled (Concentric Circles), 1973-74
Charcoal, burned forest
Location: Entre Rios, Bahia

Frenchman Pierre Verger. Verger has made a lifelong study of the connection between the religions of Africa and Brazil, the most potent incidence of convergence being in Bahia.[3]

Brazilian slavery differed from that in the United States in that it permitted the retention of the West African Yoruba culture and religion brought over by the slaves. Afro-Brazilian Candomblé devotees believe in a pantheon of sixteen Orixas. Proximity to these deities is achieved through the performance of ritual tasks, through the trance state, and through the investment of time in the community. The Candomblé community, where an extended family of initiates dwells, is a sacred space in which operates a separate, mythic reality.

Every initiation ritual involves an elaborate series of taboos. Attempts by initiates to please the Orixas with offerings of aesthetic excellence are as valuable and as commonplace as animal sacrifices. In the trance experience central to the religion, initiates manipulate sacred liturgical objects imbued with the power of the deities and incorporate special body postures and behaviors.[4]

The late Casimiro Xavier de Mendonça noted that, in creating his portraits, Cravo Neto uses everything that belongs in his closest personal domain—his domestic surroundings, natural light, family members, neighbors and spiritual guides.[5] His models are always intimates, and Cravo Neto imposes no persona on them. Nor does he calculate a photograph's outcome before the exposure. A collaborative process, the photograph is fruit of an exchange between the photographer, his human subject and a third agent—whether pheasant, stone, tortoise or African idol. The photographs can be seen as aesthetic records of transitory rituals performed in a studio environment.

Ritual performance has been an integral part of the artist's work since the early 1970s when he enacted interferences in nature using the element of fire. In one piece he marked in the jungle large, concentric circles out of huge chunks of black coal. Setting the coal on fire, allowing it to turn to white ash on the dark, charred earth, Cravo Neto revealed the aesthetic beauty of his symbology as well as the transformative power of the artistic process. Moreover, as with all his work, the piece centered on the relationship between man and tropical nature. During this period, photography played an important documentary, only minimally aesthetic role in the artist's sculptural process.

The interaction between Cravo Neto's photography and sculpture has always been substantial. He is the son of the nationally prominent sculptor Mario Cravo, who was especially influential in Brazil during the 1950s and 1960s. Early on, he made welded sculpture and assemblage in his father's studio. On an extended family residency in West Berlin in 1964, he picked up photography. Since then a prolific documentary color photographer (he has published several books), he is now working on photographic and video series exploring the cultures of the Amazon region and Bahian carnival. Cravo Neto's black and white studio photography has gained him an international following.

Along with his work in photography, Cravo Neto has continued to make consistent and provocative sculptural statements. His materials have been rusted corrugated metal, corroded steel, zinc, stone, rubber and fragments

Interference in Nature, 1970

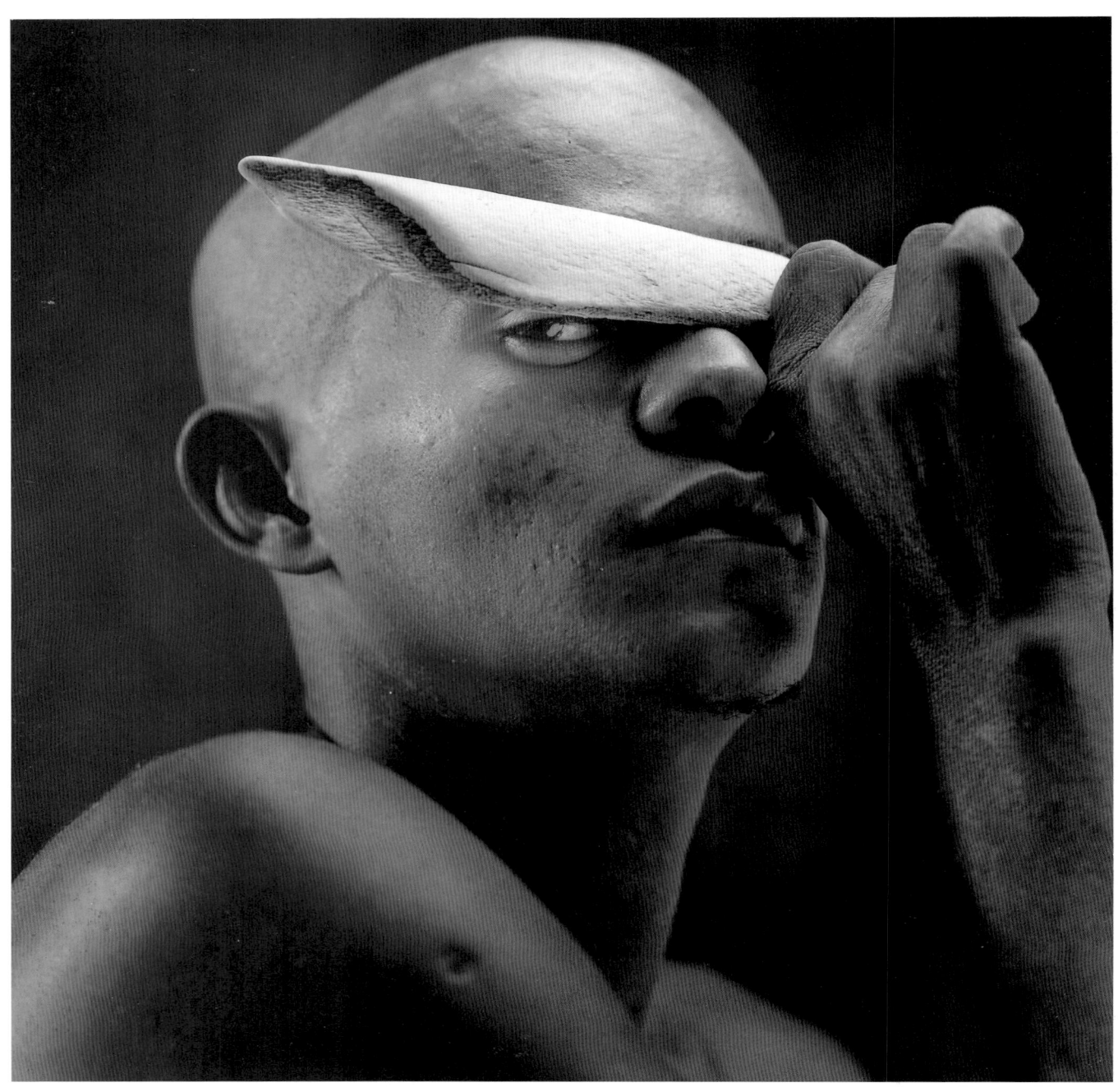

Tinho with Bone, 1990
Photograph

Man with Two Fish, 1992
Photograph

Landscape for the Future, 1986
Found copper
Collection of the artist

Untitled, 1973-74
Installation, Salvador, Bahia

Untitled, 1982
Installation, Salvador, Bahia

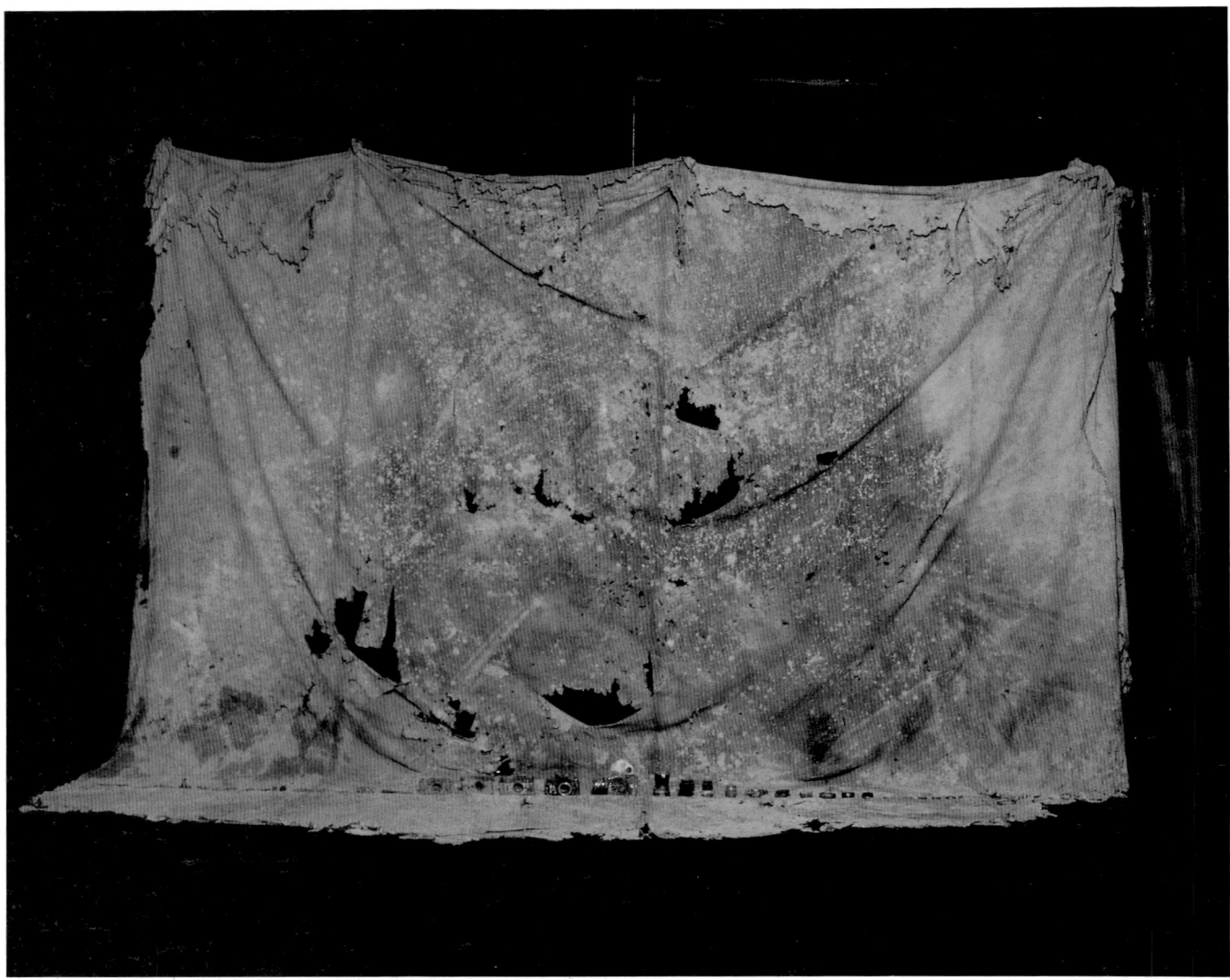

Untitled, 1980
Installation, Salvador, Bahia
Burned camera parts and tarpaulins
Collection of the artist

of the soiled and fragile truck tarpaulins he uses to provide the backdrop for his photographs. He has also created a series of powerful and poetic installation-tableaux featuring found objects. For the XIV Bienal in São Paulo in 1977, he placed a delicate bird's nest against a vertical backdrop of truck tarpaulins. Made of fiberglass filaments, the nest was a poignant statement of the interaction between nature and man, the fusion of the technological and the organic. The simple statement of the poetic nest against the tones and textures of the massive tarpaulin fragments mirrored the brooding darkness of Cravo Neto's photographic oeuvre.

For his installation at Fisher Gallery, *Scars of Our Inheritance #3,* Cravo Neto presents for the first time an idea he has been brewing for months. Onto the four walls of one gallery he projects floor-to-ceiling images of his photographs in a continuous sequence of slides, their rhythm established by sound. Charging the photographs with new meaning and kinetic life, the installation reenacts Mario Cravo Neto's intense and powerful world of ritual, conveying the temperament and passion of Bahian cultural and religious roots. As the artist himself has stated about his photographs: "The contemplative and dramatic visages presented are the scars of our inheritance."[6]

Untitled, 1977
Installation, XIV Bienal, São Paulo
Fiberglass bird's nest with tarpaulins
Collection of the artist

The Alchemy of Sexuality

TUNGA

Recurrent in Tunga's work is the ubiquitous hermetic symbol of the *ouroboros,* the snake devouring its own tail, a symbol of circular movement in which there is repetitious dissolving, evaporating, distilling and refining of matter.[1] Tunga's installations, videos, performances and objects are similarly linked by an inner relationship which causes them to echo in one another. As Guy Brett has eloquently stated: "What one experiences as the disorienting and baffling element in Tunga's work seems to me to be his search...for another order of relationship in which one body is immersed in another. Rings which are simultaneously traces of circular motion, which are femur bones, which are snakes biting their tales, which are plaits of hair, which are magnetic force-field, and so on."[2] None of Tunga's works exist in time as separate entities. They are woven together into an intricate, quasi-mythical, existential realm.

In his large-scale environmental pieces such as *Lezarts* and *Palindromo Incesto,* Tunga creates a hermetic container or "magnetosphere" from which matter is not allowed to escape but within which it endlessly circulates. He constructs a magnetically charged space by introducing three tons of shattered magnets into the exhibition space, creating a physical force field that invisibly sustains the work of art. Thick braids of copper wire, like phantasmagoric plaits of human hair, act as conductors. Organized within the space is a system of grates and grids (like giant combs) and holding pools through which the electricity or invisible forces pass. He creates a new order of kinetic sculpture—sculpture that is internally, or invisibly active only.

Because of the hermetic nature of these enormous containers, Tunga's installations can be seen as referring to the imprisonment of sexuality or to the repressed nature of bodily experience. According to Ronaldo Brito, the development of Tunga's work "obeys the logic of sexuality...tries to reproduce it metaphoricaly in terms of condensations, fusions, heatings...."[3] Rather than focusing on the psychology of sex, however, Tunga's work suggests a type of accumulator in which energy is stored and constantly

Torus, 1983
Iron
Collection of the artist

renewed. Brito indicated this function for the work as well: "...to externalize desire, balance and recycle its period of vitality."[4] In short, it is the alchemy of sexuality that Tunga's work addresses.

The ouroboros symbol, that of the snake devouring itself, is an alchemical symbol. The lessons of alchemy, the process of turning coarse materials into finer, are helpful to an understanding of Tunga's installation work. The alchemical process "is based upon complex sequences of anthropomorphizations of inanimate substances; the world and all its components are potentially infused with life.

Alchemical symbolism is rife with sexual dualisms proceeding from the fundamental opposition of two complementary anthropomorphic principles: the active, male principle...and the passive, female principle...."[5]

The work is in fact a complex metaphor for the human body as a field for the continuous interaction of processes. The human body is often inferred "by references which change drastically in scale (for example, from molar to mountain), and weave in and out between named entities (hair, comb, brain) and orderly or chaotic force-fields (magnetized fragments, plaited or loose wire) in such

Les Bijoux de Madame de Sade, 1983
Bronze

ways as to immerse the human body in myriads of other physical and notional bodies."[6] Tunga studies the relationship between sculptural energies and the sexual energies of the human body. In the video *O Nervo de Prata*, made with the filmaker Artur Omar, Tunga emphasizes the eroticism of space by repeatedly using the metaphor of swallowing.

Tunga externalizes inner processes, creating mechanisms that suggest a new order of functioning. His "refineries" are like the experiments of a mad scientist, experiments very often "exuberantly prepared for failure."[7] This does not seem to bother Tunga, who is unshaken by the chaos that is bound to intercede at any moment, by the aspect of his work that is like a machine out of control. Although he by and large uses ordinary materials such as magnets, copper wire and cast iron, these materials have become rare in post-industrial societies and present a hidden threat to technological societies. This seems to be an unforeseen by-product of the work rather than calculated by Tunga. One wonders, though, if he does not purposefully skew his experiments, causing us to question our preconcieved notions and faith in objectivity.

His materials have a very strong physical presence. Three tons of magnets concentrated in a small space cause a minimal "magnetic storm." Slight physical disturbances occur in those wearing pacemakers, difficulties arise in

Beetles' Treasure, 1992
Installation, Rio de Janeiro

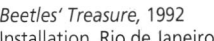

Untitled, 1990
Installation, Glasgow

computers used in the vicinity of the piece. "The force of magnetism...is presented... in an elemental, uncontrolled and disorderly form."[8] Brito has pointed out that "from the point of view of everyday reason...the choice of these materials and the processes they are subject to appear arbitrary, if not absurd. The sequence of the work is close to a delirium, or of a blind eschatalogical exploration."[9] Tunga often uses copper wire, the ultimate conducting metal, evoking an image of luxuriant hair, which in myth usually indicates that the instincts have run to excess. As the English critic Marina Warner points out, Tunga's work shares much in common with a Surrealist collage novel by Max Ernst, *Reve d'une petite fille qui roulat entrer au Carmel (A Little Girl Dreams of Taking the Veil)*. Throughout the piece, "Ernst plays on the analogies of hair, with water, with flux, with turmoil and erotic outpouring."[10]

Since 1974, Tunga has been organizing his work as projects rather than working on discrete sculptural pieces, creating performances, photographic works and videos organized around a continuing, central theme. The performance that Tunga creates for Fisher Gallery, *Viperine Vanguard*, uses live snakes as the material of art.

The international trend in contemporary art to use insects, animals and other living beings has been a salient feature of Brazilian artistic practice for over twenty years. Lygia Pape began using living creatures as early as 1967. In *Cockroach Box* she secured large, dead cockroaches to the bottom of a mirrored, acrylic box measuring one foot square by seven inches deep. Along with this collection of impaled specimens, she exhibited the *Ant Box*, a similarly constructed box in which she placed a piece of fresh meat within a series of concentric circles, allowing throngs of living, oversize ants to swarm over the meat. The first was a critique of the "mummified" art of museums, the second a statement about lust and "the unforeseeable behavior of living things."[11]

In *Viperine Vanguard,* Tunga satisfies his penchant for pseudo-scientific experimentation, and probes into the lost unity between science and art. Tunga frequently adopts the persona of a scientist (á la Jules Verne), blurring the borders between the plausible and the implausible when he does so. According to the artist, he has published material in the psychiatric journal *Rivirão—Revista de Practica Freudiana* (Rio de Janeiro, 1985), where he addressed the discovery of Siamese twins joined by long tresses of hair. He also reportedly attended a scientific congress in 1983, presenting a mock scientific paper, *"Desvios Socio-Biológicos em Espécimes Bothrops" (Socio-Biological Diversions in Bothrops Specimens).* Tunga makes renewed reference to this research in his performance *Viperine Vanguard.*

The artist's snakes (anesthetized by a professional and then braided with Tunga's assistance) are presented to the viewer as a startling scientific discovery. Mutually predatory snakes, having braided themselves together, exhibit a behavioral abnormality of a socio-biological sort. Presented in a pristine, pseudo-laboratory environment constructed within the gallery space, the viewer is protected from all harm from the "poisonous," aberrant snakes by a tall glass enclosure.

This glass-enclosure with braided snakes is an alternate version of the alchemical ouroboros or Tunga's magnetosphere. It, too, contains a fluid force-field linking the primordial with the scientific and posing a hidden menace, as the snakes may awaken out of their deep

Lezart 5, 1989
Installation, Chicago
Detail

Lezart 2, 1989
Installation, Kortrijk, Belgium
Copper, steel, iron and magnets

Lezart 2, 1989
Installation, Kortrijk, Belgium
Detail

Lezart 1, 1989
Installation, London
Detail

Lezart 2, 1989
Installation, Kortrijk, Belgium
Copper, steel, iron and magnets

lethargy at any moment. Within the private confines of the gallery space, and mimicking the customary Western scientific mode of examination from a safe vantage point, we are invited to witness "the other": the capturing and ordering of elemental Brazil, a touch of the Amazonian sublime. Tunga evoked similar issues of environmental and cultural exploitation in an exhibition at the Cornerhouse in Manchester, England, in 1990 by "making a heavy plait" out of huge coils of copper wire "tied with a frivolous bow, but lopped, like a trophy of a hunted enemy."[12]

Tunga presents his snakes in a suitably anesthetic environment, complete with computer moniter. The audible ticking of the screen as it continuously displays a mysterious viperine "code" devised by Tunga, is like a ritual incantation or abracadabra, as well as a parody of scientific procedure. Tunga, who subverts meaning by associating discrepant sensory experience with narrative information, consistently foils our notion of logic and sense of distance. Much of his work is about the limits of reason.

Tunga's source material is seemingly without boundaries. Exploring the disciplines of religion, science, art and philosophy, he discovers between them trenchant analogies and continuities. An inveterate storyteller, Tunga often makes reference to an apocryphal tale by St. Augustine, a story his father, the poet Gerardo Mello Mourão, told him as a child. St. Augustine was at the edge of the sea, trying to understand the mystery of the Trinity using all his powers of reason. Absorbed in thought he noticed the presence of a child nearby who repeatedly went to the edge of the sea, filled a thimble full of salt water, then returned to the beach and poured the seawater into a small hole in the sand. St. Augustine approached the child and asked about the activity. The child responded by saying that he was transferring the ocean to the hole. When St. Augustine pointed out the futility of the deed, the boy responded, "More futile are those who try to understand the mystery of the Trinity using base reason." Then the child—or angel, conjectures Tunga—disappeared.

Tunga became interested anew in the Catholic philosopher and saint while studying Wittgenstein's discussions about the limits of language. St. Augustine's tale, about the limits of reason, is certainly pertinent to Tunga's work, which suggests the path of direct physical and sensorial experience. The Brazilian critic Paulo Sergio Duarte notes that "Tunga's poetics—is not aimed exclusively at the eye, as certain musical compositions are not aimed exclusively at the ear: [the work] engages body and soul, matter and spirit, the whole 'being.'"[13]

Tunga transmits his ideas through the skin, through the sensations. One understands the work at the visceral level, the instinctive level, experiences it as disgust, as inner awe, as something offensive yet sublime. In the externalization of visceral internal experiences, Tunga often calls forth feelings of horror tinged with pleasure—as revealed through the experience of elemental chaos and the forceful energy of Brazilian nature. Like the work of the artist Lygia Pape, Tunga's work is "neither concepts nor preconceptions, but rather a fragmentation of sensations that leads...from a space to an event to a state."[14]

4731 - D.454 - FT. 76/77/69/105-

CORRESPONDÊNCIA

Foto Lúcia Zaremba

DESVIÓS SOCIO-BIOLÓGICOS EM ESPÉCIMES BOTHROPS

por M. Sebescen*

A partir de 82, por cinco anos podemos observar o confronto de bothrops mútuo-predadoras.
As pesquisas descritas foram realizadas em habitat natural (evitando desvios adaptacionais) visando a compreensão de um comportamento extraordinário, por nós descoberto, de Muçuranas albinas e Jararacas filhotes.

Dos desvios
Estando muçuranas albinas fora do período nutricional, uma delas depara-se a um par de Jararacas não-adultas, ao invés de travar combate, observa a rival por até 30 minutos para em seguida formar uma *trança absolutamente regular* e nessa postura entrar em profundo letargo por extenso período. A cada trança de cobras formada, faz-se notar uma série de peculiaridades, a saber.

Teoria geral do desvio comportamental.
As características gerais indicam que esse desvio se

(cont. pg. 243 vol II)

Socio-Biological Diversions in Bothrops Specimens, 1983
Printing on paper

ENDNOTES

Introduction

1. Steve Proffitt, "Wallace Stegner: Environmentalism Remains the Key for the Enigmatic California Writer," *Los Angeles Times* (June 7, 1992): M3.
2. Ibid.
3. In fact, the first definitive exhibition of Neo-Concrete art was held in 1959 in Rio de Janeiro, the same year that Jules Langsner held the important exhibition "Abstract Classicists" at Los Angeles County Museum of Art. The show included the Geometric Abstraction of John McLaughlin, among others, and first defined a new direction for American art that resulted in Minimalism.
4. Cathy de Zegher, "Ver," *"Lezarts" by Tunga/"Through" by Cildo Meireles* (Kortrijk, Belgium: The Kanaal Art Foundation, 1989), n.p.
5. Paulo Venancio Filho, *"Lezarts" by Tunga/"Through" by Cildo Meireles* (Kortrijk, Belgium: The Kanaal Art Foundation, 1989), n.p.
6. Frederico Morais, *Pequeno Roteiro Cronólogico das Invenções de Helio Oiticica* (Rio De Janeiro, 1980), 2.
7. Guy Brett, *Transcontinental* (London: Verso, in association with Ikon Gallery, Manchester, 1990), 9.
8. Frederico Morais, "Brazil: International Languages," *Brazil Projects* (New York: P.S.1, The Institute for Art and Urban Resources, Inc., in association with the Sociedade Cultural Arte Brasil, São Paulo, 1988), 30.
9. Ronaldo Brito, *Neoconcretismo, Vértice e Ruptura* (Rio de Janeiro, Funarte, 1985) quoted in Guy Brett, "Art & National Identity: A Critics' Symposium," *Art in America* 79, no. 9 (September 1991): 115.
10. Brett, *Transcontinental*, 30.

The Consumption of Paradise

1. Cildo Meireles in Antonio Manuel, *Ondas do Corpo*, reprinted in Ronaldo Brito and Eudoro Augusto Macieira de Sousa, *Cildo Meireles* (Rio de Janeiro: Funarte, 1981), 24.
2. Cultural repression took many forms—books were banned, seized and burned. Hundreds of artists and writers were harrassed, imprisoned and even tortured. Consequently there was a general self-imposed exile from Brazil by intellectuals and scientists. Darcy Ribeiro, *Aos Trancos e Barrancos: Como o Brasil Deu no que Deu* (Rio de Janeiro: Editora Guanabara, 1985), 1825-1833.
3. Guy Brett, "Cildo Meireles," *"Lezarts" by Tunga/"Through" by Cildo Meireles* (Kortrijk, Belgium: The Kanaal Art Foundation, 1989), n.p.
4. Brett, *Transcontinental*, 47.
5. Lawrence Weschler, "Cildo Meireles: Cries from the Wilderness," *Art News* 89, no. 6 (Summer 1990): 96,98.
6. Brett, *"Lezarts" by Tunga/"Through" by Cildo Meireles*, n.p.
7. Lu Menezes, "How to Build Troubled Skies" (Rio de Janeiro, 1990), reprinted in *Transcontinental*, 40.
8. Weschler, "Cries from the Wilderness," 95-98.
9. Cildo Meireles, "Bric-a-Brac," Brasilia, 1986 in *"Lezarts" by Tunga/"Through" by Cildo Meireles,* n.p.

Scars of Our Inheritance

1. Edward Leffingwell, "Report from Brazil: São Paulo Diary," *Art in America* 77, no. 1 (January 1989): 59.
2. Margarida Medeiros, "Entre a sonho e o símbolo," Lisbon *Público* (April 12, 1992): 35.
3. "Mario Cravo e Pierre Verger Mostram a Bahia sobre a montanha, penetrada de mar," *Correio da Bahia* (September 17, 1979): Sec. 2, 1.
4. Mikelle Smith Omari, *From the Inside to the Outside: The Art and Ritual of Bahian Candomblé* (Los Angeles: The University of California, 1984), 12-19. According to Omari, Candomblé is a distinct subculture peripheral to the European and American-oriented sectors of the Bahian culture which relegate blacks to an inferior position socially, economically and politically. Candomblé society, which is not based on principles of Western capitalism, extols community, rather than private property. The central function of the Candomblé is mutual aid, both spiritual and economic. Though it is primarily an Afro-Brazilian phenomenon, a significant number of whites participate in the religion.
5. Casimiro Xavier de Mendonça, *Mario Cravo Neto* (São Paulo: Galeria Arco Arte Contemporânea, 1989), n.p.
6. Unpublished written statement by the artist.

The Alchemy of Sexuality

1. John F. Moffitt, "Marcel Duchamp: Alchemist of the Avant-Garde," *The Spiritual in Art: Abstract Painting 1890-1985* (Los Angeles: Los Angeles County Museum of Art, 1986), 264.
2. Brett, *"Lezarts" by Tunga/"Through" by Cildo Meireles*, n.p.
3. Ronaldo Brito, "Transparencia do Desejo," exh. broch. (Rio de Janeiro, 1987), n.p.
4. Ronaldo Brito, *O Mar a Pele* (Rio de Janeiro: Pano de Pó, 1989), n.p.
5. Moffitt, "Marcel Duchamp," 259-260.
6. Brett, *Transcontinental*, 38.
7. *Tunga* (Glasgow, Scotland: Third Eye Centre, 1990), n.p.
8. Brett, *"Lezarts" by Tunga/"Through" by Cildo Meireles*, n.p.
9. Brito, *Desejo*, n.p.
10. Marina Warner, "Bush Natural," *Parkett* 27 (1991): 7.
11. Lygia Pape, *Lygia Pape* (Rio de Janeiro: Funarte, 1983), 46.
12. Warner, "Bush Natural," 10.
13. Paulo Sergio Duarte, "Tunga's Poetics," *Tunga* (Chicago: The Museum of Contemporary Art, 1989), n.p.
14. Mario Pedroso, *Lygia Pape* (Rio de Janeiro: Funarte, 1983), 1.

ARTISTS' BIOGRAPHIES

Cildo Meireles

1948 Born in Rio de Janeiro.

Education

1963 Studied with Peruvian artist Felix Alejandro Barrenechea Avilez, Brasilia.

1968 National School of Fine Arts, Rio de Janeiro.

Selected Individual Exhibitions

1967 Museu de Arte Moderna da Bahia, Salvador.

1975 Museu de Arte Moderna, Rio de Janeiro. Galeria Luiz Buarque de Hollanda e Paulo Bittencourt, Rio de Janeiro.

1977 Museu de Arte e Cultura Popular, Cuiabá.

1978 "Cildo Meireles: Drawings from the Luis Buarque de Hollanda and Paulo Bittencourt Collection," Pinacoteca do Estado de São Paulo.

1979 "The Sermon of the Mountain: Fiat Lux," Centro Cultural Cândido Mendes, Rio de Janeiro.
Galeria Saramenha, Rio de Janeiro.

1981 Galeria Luisa Strina, São Paulo.

1983 "Obscure Light," Galeria Saramenha, Rio de Janeiro and Galeria Luisa Strina, São Paulo.
"Eureka/Blindhotland," installation at Rio Arte Humaitá, Rio de Janeiro.

1984 "Red Shift," Museu de Arte Moderna, Rio de Janeiro.
"Two Collections" (drawings), Sala Oswaldo Goeldi, Brasilia.

1986 Galeria Luisa Strina, São Paulo and Petite Galerie do Rio de Janeiro.
"Red Shift," Museu de Arte Contemporânea, University of São Paulo, São Paulo.

1990 "Cildo Meireles," The Museum of Modern Art, New York.
The Institute of Contemporary Art, London.

1992 Galeria Luiza Strina, São Paulo.

Selected Group Exhibitions

1965 II Salão de Arte Moderna do Distrito Federal.

1970 "Information," The Museum of Modern Art, New York.
Petite Galerie, Rio de Janeiro.
Palacio das Artes, Belo Horizonte.

1973 "Expo-Projeção," Galeria Grife, São Paulo.

1976 "International Actuality," Venice Biennale.

1977 Paris Biennale.

1979 Núcleo de Arte Contemporânea, João Pessoa, Paraiba.

1981 Museum of Modern Art, Medellin, Colombia.
XVI Bienal Internacional de São Paulo.
"From Modern Art to Contemporary Art," Museu de Arte Moderna, Rio de Janeiro.

1982 "From Modern Art to Contemporary Art," Calouste Gulbenkian Foundation, Lisbon, Portugal.

1983 Sul America, Rio de Janeiro.

1984 V Sydney Biennale, Sydney, Australia.

1987 Museu de Arte Contemporânea, São Paulo.
"Massão/Missões" (How to Build Cathedrals) installation in Brasilia, Rio de Janeiro, and São Paulo.
"Vision of the Artist," National Theater, Brasilia; Parque Lage, Rio de Janeiro; and Museu de Arte do Estado de São Paulo.
"Modernity: Brasilian Art in the 20th Century," Museé d'Art Moderne, Paris and Museu de Arte Moderna, São Paulo.

1988 "Brazil Projects," P.S. 1/Institute for Art and Urban Resources, New York.
"The Latin American Spirit," The Bronx Museum, New York.
Exit Art, New York.

1989 The Kanaal Art Foundation, Kortrijk, Belgium.
"Magiciens de la Terre," Centre Georges Pompidou, Paris.
Galeria Luisa Strina, São Paulo.
XX Bienal Internacional de São Paulo.

1990 "The Rhetorical Image," The New Museum of Contemporary Art, New York.
"Transcontinental," Ikon Gallery, Birmingham and Cornerhouse, Manchester, England.

1991 "Denonciation," School of Architecture of Normandy, France.

1992 "Documenta," Kassel.
"Pour la Suite du Monde," Musée d'Art Contemporaine, Montreal.
"America, Bride of the Sun," Royal Museum of Fine Arts, Antwerp.
"Encounters/Displacements," Archer M. Huntington Art Gallery, University of Texas at Austin.

1993 "Body to Earth," Fisher Gallery, University of Southern California, Los Angeles.

Videos and Films

"Cildo Meireles," 35mm color, 11 minutes. Written and directed by Wilson Coutinho; produced by Luis Alberto Lira.

"Le faux monnayeur," color, 6 minutes. Directed by Frédéric Laffont R.T.F./Antenne II.

"Red Shift," color, 16 minutes. Directed by Tuca Morais.

Mario Cravo Neto

1947 Born in Salvador, Bahia.

Education

1963 First studied drawing, sculpture, and photography with his father, the sculptor Mario Cravo, Jr.

1964 Studied photography with Hans Mann in Berlin.

1970 Studied sculpture with Jack Krueger at the Art Students League, New York.

Selected Individual Exhibitions

1971 Galeria Documenta, São Paulo.
Museu de Arte Moderna da Bahia, Salvador.

XI Bienal Internacional de São Paulo.
1972 Galeria Grupo B, Rio de Janeiro.
Galeria Documenta, São Paulo.
New York City Public Library, Hudson Branch, New York.
1973 Galeria Documenta, São Paulo.
Galeria de Arte da Bahia, Salvador.
XII Bienal Internacional de São Paulo.
1975 XIII Bienal Internacional de São Paulo.
1976 Modern Art Gallery, Munich (with Mario Cravo, Jr.).
Museu de Arte Moderna da Bahia, Salvador (with Vicente Sampaio Neto).
Hovedgaard, Hillerod, Denmark.
1977 Galeria Múltipla, São Paulo.
XIV Bienal Internacional de São Paulo.
1979 Museu de Arte da Bahia, Salvador (with Pierre Verger).
Museu de Arte de São Paulo (with Pierre Verger).
1982 Brazilian American Cultural Institute, Washington, D.C.
1983 Galleria Il Diaframma/Canon, Milan.
Museu de Arte de São Paulo.
Galeria Arco Arte Contemporânea, São Paulo.
XVII Bienal Internacional de São Paulo.
1984 Museu de Arte Moderna, Rio de Janeiro.
Fotografia Oltre, Chiasso.
1987 Vision Gallery, San Francisco.
Billechusets Gallery, Copenhagen.
1988 Suomen Valokuvataiteen Museo, Helsinki.
Palazzo Fortuny, Venice (with Miguel Rio Branco).
1990 Springer Gallery, Berlin.
Canon Image Center, Amsterdam.
1991 Foto Galeria del Teatro Municipal General San Martin, Buenos Aires.
ACF Galeria de Arte, Salvador.
1992 Houston FotoFest, Houston.
Galeria Módulo, Lisbon.
Fahey/Klein Gallery, Los Angeles.
Witkin Gallery, New York.

Selected Group Exhibitions
1965 I Bienal de Artes Plásticas da Bahia, Salvador.
1968 90 Anos da Escola de Belas Artes da Universidade Federal de Bahia, Salvador.
II Salão Baiano da Fotografia Contemporânea, Salvador.
1970 Soho Artists Festival, New York.
"Le Latin American Artists," Andres Bello Auditorium, Washington, D.C.
1972 "Panorama da Arte Brasileira Atual," Museu de Arte Moderna de São Paulo.
"Arte Baiana Hoje," Museu de Arte Moderna da Bahia, Salvador and Hotel Miramar, Recife.
"Brasil Plástica 72," Fundação Bienal de São Paulo.
"Arte/Brasil/Hoje: 50 Anos Depois," Galeria Collectio, São Paulo.
1973 Galeria Vernissage, Rio de Janeiro.
Galeria Berlinda, Salvador.
"Expo-Projeção 73," Galeria Grife, São Paulo—Centro de Arte y Comunicacion, Buenos Aires, Argentina.
"22 Artistas Baianos," Fundação Patrimônio Artístico e Cultural da Bahia, Salvador.
1974 "Brasil 74," Centro de Arte y Comunicacion, La Plata and Buenos Aires, Argentina.
"Art Systems in Latin America," Institute of Contemporary Art, London; L'Espace Pierre Cardin, Paris; and Galleria Civica D'Arte Moderna, Ferrára.
1975 "Artistas Contemporâneos," Escola de Belas Artes da Universidade Federal da Bahia, Salvador.
"Four Artists from Bahia," Art Gallery of the Brazilian-American Cultural Institute, Washington, D.C.
"Panorama da Arte Atual Brasileira," Museu de Arte Moderna de São Paulo.
1980 Salone Internazionale della Cinematografia, Ottica e Fotografia (SICOF), Milan.
1981 "Fotografia Lateinamerika," Künsthaus Zürich and Akademia der Künst, Berlin.
"Panorama 81," Museu de Arte Moderna, São Paulo.
1983 "Brazilian Photography, Six Contemporaries," The Photographer's Gallery, London.
"Bresil des bresiliens," Centre Georges Pompidou, Paris.
1985 I Quadrienal de Fotografia, Museu de Arte Moderna, São Paulo.
"A Arte e Seus Materiais: Atitudes Contemporâneas," Galeria Sergio Millet, Funarte, Rio de Janeiro.
"Panorama da Arte Atual Brasileira," Museu de Arte Moderna, São Paulo.
"50 Years of Color," Círculo de Belas Artes, Madrid.
1988 "Het Portret," Canon Image Center, Amsterdam.
"Brazil Projects," P.S.1/Institute for Art and Urban Resources, New York.
"Splendeus et misere du corps," Museé d'art et d'historie de Fribourg and Museé d'art Moderne de La Ville de Paris (Triennale Internat. de La Photografie-Mois de la Photo).
1989 "Realites Magiques," Photografie Latino Americaine Contemporaine, Museet for Fotokunst, Odense and Museum Voor Fotografie, Antwerp.
1991 "13 Photographers," Witkin Gallery, New York.
"Incursão pelo Imaginário na Fotografia Brasileira Contemporânea," Rencontres Internationales de La Photographie, Arles.
1992 "Arte Amazonas," Museu de Arte Moderna, Rio de

Janeiro; Museu de Arte de Brasilia; Bienal de São Paulo; and Staatliche Kunsthalle, Berlin.

1993 "Body to Earth," Fisher Gallery, University of Southern California, Los Angeles.

Videos and Films
1975 "Ubirajara," 35mm. Directed by André Luis Oliveira (Feature).
1978 "Smetek," 16mm. Directed by Walter Lima (Documentary).
1978 "Nós," 16mm. Directed by Walter Lima (Short Fiction).
1979 "Iya-Mi-Agbá: The Sacred Space," Directed by Juana Elbain (Documentary).
1990 "GW-43, Gulf War," 20 minutes.
1991 "NASH, U 19-AMAZONIA," 20 minutes.

Tunga
1952 Born in Palmares, Pernambuco (Brazil).

Education
1974 School of Architecture, Universidade Santa Úrsula, Rio de Janeiro.

Selected Individual Exhibitions
1973 Instituto de Arte de la Universidade Católica del Valparaiso, Chile.
1974 Museu de Arte Moderna, Rio de Janeiro.
1975 Museu de Arte Moderna, Rio de Janeiro.
1976 Galeria Luisa Strina, São Paulo.
1979 Nucleo de Arte Contemporânea, Paraiba.
Centro Cultural Cândido Mendes, Rio de Janeiro.
Mabe Gallery, New York.
1980 Espaço ABC (Arte Brasileira Contemporânea), Rio de Janeiro.
1981 Gabinete de Arte Raquel Arnaud, São Paulo.
1982 Centro Cultural Cândido Mendes, Rio de Janeiro.
1984 GB Galeria de Arte, Rio de Janeiro.
1985 Gabinete de Arte Raquel Arnaud, São Paulo.
1986 Galeria Saramenha, Rio de Janeiro.
Museu de Arte de Universidade Federal de Mato Grosso.
1989 The Museum of Contemporary Art, Chicago.
Whitechapel Gallery, London.
Stedelijk Museum, Amsterdam.
Galeria Paulo Klabin, Rio de Janeiro.
1990 The Power Plant, Toronto.
The Third Eye Center, Glasgow.
1991 Galeria Millan, São Paulo.
1992 Museu Nacional de Belas Artes, Rio de Janeiro.

Selected Group Exhibitions
1974 Galeria Intercontinental, Rio de Janeiro.
1975 "Panorama de Arte Atual," Museu de Arte Contemporânea de São Paulo.
1977 "Projects," National Gallery of Canada, Ottawa.
1980 Palazzo Reale, Milan.
1981 Installation, Biennial Pavilion, XVI Bienal Internacional de São Paulo.
1982 41st Bienal Internazionale di Arte, Venice.
"Coleção Gilberto Chateaubriand," Museu de Arte Moderna, Rio de Janeiro and Museu de Arte Moderno, São Paulo.
1983 Sugar Loaf, Rio de Janeiro.
Espaço Cultural Sergio Porto, Rio de Janeiro.
1984 1st Salão de Arte da Universidade Federal Fluminense.
1985 "Contemporary Art from Brazil," Hara Museum of Contemporary Art, Tokyo.
"Escultura '85," Museo Ambiental, Caracas, Venezuela.
1985 "Transvanguarda e Cultura," Museu de Arte Moderna, Rio de Janeiro.
"Escultura 85," Museo Ambiental, Caracas, Venezuela.
"Homenagem a Maria Leontina," Petite Galerie, Rio de Janeiro.
"Denison Collection," São Paulo.
"Uma Luz sobre a Cidade," Galerie UFF, Niterói.
1986 Bienal Latino Americano de Arte sobre Papel, Buenos Aires.
Museu de Arte do Rio Grande do Sul, Brazil.
1987 XIX Bienal Internacional de Arte, São Paulo.
"Imaginarios Singulares," Biennial Pavilion, São Paulo.
"Ao Colecionador," Museu de Arte Moderna do Rio de Janeiro.
"Modernity: Brasilian Art in the 20th Century," Museé d'Art Moderne, Paris and Museu de Arte Moderna, São Paulo.
1988 Museu de Arte Contemporânea, Campinas.
"Do Objeto ao Desenho," Galeria Gilberto Chateaubriand, Rio de Janeiro.
"Ponto para 21," Rio Design Center, Rio de Janeiro.
1989 The Kanaal Art Foundation, Kortrijk, Belgium.
Gabinete de Arte Raquel Arnaud, São Paulo.
"Nossos anos oitenta," Casa de Cultura Laura Alvim, Rio de Janeiro.
Galeria Saramenha, Rio de Janeiro.
Galeria ARCO, São Paulo.
1990 "Transcontinental," Cornerhouse, Manchester, United Kingdom.
1991 "Viva Brasil Viva," Kulturhusset, Stockholm.
1992 "Arte Amazonia," Museu de Arte Moderna, Rio de Janeiro.
"Latin American Artists of the Twentieth Century," Estación Plaza de Armas, Sevilla, Spain.
1993 "Body to Earth," Fisher Gallery, University of Southern California, Los Angeles.

Videos and Films
1987 "O Nervo de Prata," 20 minutes. Directed by Artur Omar. Berlin Video and Cinema Festival.

SELECTED BIBLIOGRAPHY

Amaral, Aracy. "Cravo Neto: a sociedade orgânica do amanhã." *Folha de São Paulo* (November 24, 1974).

XX Bienal Internacional de Sao Paulo. Sao Paulo: Fundacao Bienal, 1989.

XXI Bienal Internacional de São Paulo. São Paulo: Fundação Bienal, in association with Editora Marca D'Água, 1991.

Brazilian Artists in the 20th International São Paulo Biennial. São Paulo: Editora Marca D'Água, 1989.

Brazil Projects. Long Island City, New York: P.S. 1, The Institute for Art and Urban Resources, Inc. and Sociadade Cultural Arte Brasil, São Paulo, Brazil, 1988.

Brett, Guy. "Art & National Identity: A Critics' Symposium." *Art in America* 79, no. 9 (September 1991): 80+.

Brett, Guy. *Transcontinental*. London: Verso, in association with Ikon Gallery, Manchester, 1990.

Brito, Ronaldo and Eudoro Augusto Macieira de Sousa. *Cildo Meireles*. Rio de Janeiro: Funarte, 1981.

Brito, Ronaldo. *O Mar a Pele*. Rio de Janeiro: Pano de Pó, 1989.

Brito, Ronaldo. "Transparencia do Desejo," exh. broch. Rio de Janeiro, 1987.

Carluccio, Luigi. "Phil Marco, Lucien Clerque, Mario Cravo Neto." *Panorama* (January 12, 1981): 26.

Castro, Fernando and Miguel González. "FotoFest 1992." *Art Nexus* 51 (August 1992): 62-69.

Kossoy, Boris. *História Geral das Artes no Brasil*. São Paulo, 1983.

Cravo Neto, Mario. *A Cidade da Bahia*. Salvador: Áries Editora, 1984.

_____. *Cravo*. Salvador: Áries Editora, 1983.

_____. *Exvoto*. Preface by P.M. Bardi. Salvador: Áries Editora, 1986.

_____. "O Fundo Neutro." Cravo Neto. São Paulo: Galeria Arco Arte Contemporânea, 1983.

_____. *Os Estranhos Filhos da Casa*. Salvador: Áries Editora, 1985.

Doctors, Márcio. "Guy Brett: Arte Brasileira Sem Folclore." *Galeria* 14 (1989): 72-3.

Duarte, Paulo Sergio. "Tunga's Poetics." *Tunga*. Chicago: The Museum of Contemporary Art, 1989.

Leffingwell, Edward. "Report from Brazil: São Paulo Diary." *Art in America* 77, no. 1 (January 1989): 55-65.

"Lezarts" by Tunga/"Through" by Cildo Meireles. Kortrijk, Belgium: The Kanaal Art Foundation, 1989.

"Mario Cravo e Pierre Verger Mostram a Bahia sobre a montanha, penetrada de mar." *Correio da Bahia* (September 17, 1979) Sec. 2, 1.

Medeiros, Margarida. "Entre a sonho e o símbolo." *Público* (April 12, 1992), 35

_____. "Da imagem como símbolo." *Público* (April 17, 1992): 22.

Mendonça, Casimiro Xavier de. "Mario Cravo Neto." *Atlante* 1 1989).

_____. *Mario Cravo Neto*. São Paulo: Galeria Arco Arte Contemporânea, 1989.

_____. *Mario Cravo Neto*. Salvador: Áries Editora, in association with ADA Galeria de Arte, 1991.

Morais, Frederico. *Pequeno Roteiro Cronologico das Invencoes de Helio Oiticica*, Rio De Janeiro, 1980.

Mota, Carlos Guilherme. *Ideologia da Cultura Brasileira, 1933-1974*. São Paulo: Editora Atica, 1990.

Moura, João, Jr. *Cildo Meireles: Obscura Luz (Obscure Light)*. Rio de Janeiro: Galeria Saramenha, 1983.

Murray, Joan. "The Sculptural Nude." *Artweek* 18, no. 23 (June 27, 1987): 11.

Oliveira, Moracy. "Espíritos sem nome." *Fotoptica* (May 1985): 14-33.

Omari, Mikelle Smith. *From the Inside to the Outside: The Art and Ritual of Bahian Candomblé*. Los Angeles: The University of California, 1984.

Pedroso, Mario. *Lygia Pape*. Rio de Janeiro: Funarte, 1983.

Perreault, John. "A Rain Forest of Signs." *Village Voice* (April 3, 1990): 99.

Proffitt, Steve. "Wallace Stegner: Environmentalism Remains the Key for the Enigmatic California Writer." *Los Angeles Times* (June 7, 1992): M3.

Ribeiro, Darcy. *Aos Trancos e Barrancos: Como o Brasil Deu no que Deu*. Rio de Janeiro: Editora Guanabara, 1985.

Ribeiro, Leogilson. "Da natureza ao acrílico." *Veja* (June 23, 1971): 88-89.

Rocha, Wilson. *A Alma e a Máscara: Mario Cravo Neto*. Salvador: Galeria O Cavalete, 1988.

Tunga. Glasgow, Scotland: Third Eye Centre, 1990.

Warner, Marina. "Bush Natural." *Parkett* 27 (1991): 6-11.

Weschler, Lawrence. "Cildo Meireles: Cries from the Wilderness." *Art News* 89, no. 6 (Summer 1990): 95-98.